Construction Vehicles at Work

BULLDOZERS

by Kathryn Clay

CAPSTONE PRESS
a capstone imprint

Little Pebble is published by Capstone Press,
1710 Roe Crest Drive, North Mankato, Minnesota 56003
www.mycapstone.com

Library of Congress Cataloging-in-Publication Data
Names: Clay, Kathryn, author.
Title: Bulldozers / by Kathryn Clay.
Description: North Mankato, Minnesota : Capstone Press, [2017] | Series:
   Little pebble. Construction vehicles at work | Audience: Ages 4–8. |
   Audience: K to grade 3. | Includes bibliographical references and index.
Identifiers: LCCN 2015048721| ISBN 9781515725299 (library binding) |
ISBN 9781515725343 (pbk.) | ISBN 9781515725398 (ebook pdf)
Subjects: LCSH: Bulldozers—Juvenile literature. | Earthmoving machinery—Juvenile literature.
Classification: LCC TA735 .C585 2017 | DDC 629.225—dc23
LC record available at http://lccn.loc.gov/2015048721

Editorial Credits
Erika L. Shores, editor; Juliette Peters and Kayla Rossow, designers;
Eric Gohl, media researcher; Tori Abraham, production specialist

Photo Credits
Alamy: ZUMA Press Inc, 7; iStockphoto: kozmoat98, 9; Shutterstock: artiomp, cover, bogdanhoda, 11, f9photos, 5, TFoxFoto, 1, 13, 15, 17, 19, Vadim Ratnikov, 21

Design elements: Shutterstock

Printed and bound in the United States of America.
010577R

Table of Contents

About Bulldozers

Look!

Here comes a bulldozer.

Lee is the driver.

He sits in the cab.

cab

Here is the blade.

It pushes dirt.

blade

The blade is strong.

It is steel.

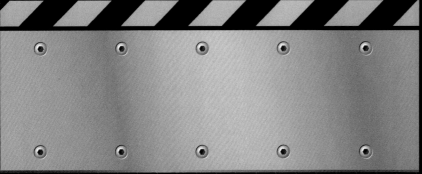

Here are the tracks.

There are two.

track

track

Tracks go over hills.

Tracks go through mud.

At Work

Thud!

Clear a path.

Push down trees.

Rocks and sand get

pushed away.

Now the land is flat.

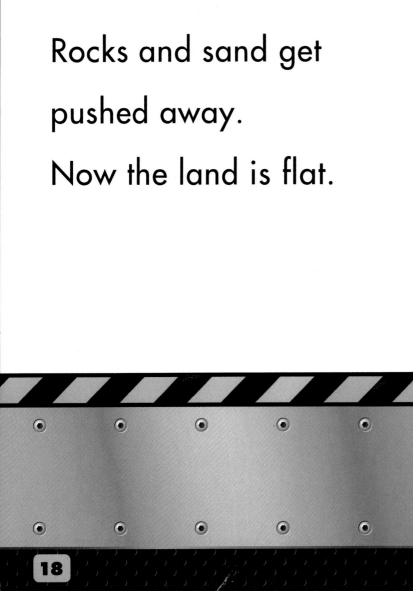

Here is the new road.

Nice job, bulldozer!

Glossary

blade—a wide, curved piece of metal; the blade pushes or scrapes rocks and dirt

cab—the place where the driver sits

track—a metal belt that runs around wheels

Read More

Hayes, Amy. *Big Bulldozers.* Machines that Work. New York: Cavendish Square Publishing, 2016.

Lennie, Charles. *Bulldozers.* Construction Machines. Minneapolis: Abdo Kids, 2015.

Osier, Dan. *Bulldozers.* Construction Site. New York: PowerKids Press, 2014.

Internet Sites

FactHound offers a safe, fun way to find Internet sites related to this book. All of the sites on FactHound have been researched by our staff.

Here's all you do:
Visit *www.facthound.com*
Type in this code: 9781515725299

Check out projects, games and lots more at
www.capstonekids.com

Index